Discretionary Budget Authority by Subfunction: An Overview

D. Andrew Austin

Analyst in Economic Policy

April 25, 2013

Congressional Research Service

7-5700

www.crs.gov

R41726

Summary

President Obama's FY2014 budget submission was released on April 10, 2013. Using data from that budget submission, this report provides a graphical overview of historical trends in discretionary budget authority (BA) from FY1976 through FY2012, preliminary estimates for FY2013 spending, and the levels consistent with the President's proposals for FY2014 through FY2018. Spending caps and budget enforcement mechanisms established in the Budget Control Act of 2011 (P.L. 112-25; BCA) strongly affected the FY2013 budget cycle and are likely to shape the FY2014 budget cycle as well. BCA provisions include separate caps on discretionary defense and non-defense spending.

As the 113th Congress considers funding levels for FY2014 and beyond, past spending trends may prove useful in framing policy discussions. For example, rapid growth in national defense and other security spending in the past decade has played an important role in fiscal discussions. The American Recovery and Reinvestment Act of 2009 (P.L. 111-5; ARRA) funded sharp increases in spending on education, energy, and other areas. Since FY2010, however, base defense discretionary spending has essentially been held flat and non-defense discretionary spending has been reduced significantly. The base defense budget excludes war funding (Overseas Contingency Operations/Global War on Terror). This report may provide a starting point for discussions about spending trends and federal priorities, but it does not attempt to explain spending patterns in each policy area. Other CRS products are available to provide insights into those spending trends in specific functional areas.

Functional categories (e.g., national defense, agriculture, etc.) provide a means to compare federal funding for activities within broad policy areas that often cut across several federal agencies. Subfunction categories provide a finer division of funding levels within narrower policy areas. Budget function categories are used within the budget resolution and for other purposes, such as possible program cuts and tax expenditures. Three functions, however, are omitted. These are (1) allowances, which contain items reflecting technical budget adjustments; (2) net interest, which by its nature is not discretionary spending; and (3) undistributed offsetting receipts, which are treated for federal budgetary purposes as negative budget authority.

Spending in this report is measured and illustrated in terms of discretionary budget authority as a percentage of gross domestic product (GDP). Measuring spending as a percentage of GDP in effect controls for inflation and population increases. A flat line on such graphs indicates that spending in that category is increasing at the same rate as overall economic growth.

Discretionary spending is provided and controlled through appropriations acts, which provide budget authority to federal agencies to fund many of the activities commonly associated with such federal government functions as running executive branch agencies, congressional offices and agencies, and international operations of the government. Essentially all spending on federal wages and salaries is discretionary. Program administration costs for entitlement programs such as Social Security are generally funded by discretionary spending, while mandatory spending generally funds the benefits provided through those programs. Thus, the figures showing trends in discretionary budget authority presented herein do not reflect the much larger expenditures on program benefits supported by mandatory spending. For some federal agencies, such as the Departments of Veterans Affairs and Transportation, the division of expenditures into discretionary and mandatory categories can be complex. This report will not be updated.

Contents

Figures

Tables

Contacts

T his report presents figures showing trends in discretionary budget authority as a percentage of GDP by subfunction within each of 17 budget function categories, using data from President Obama's FY2014 budget submission.[1] This report provides a graphical overview of historical trends in discretionary budget authority from FY1976 through FY2012, preliminary estimates for FY2013 spending, and the levels consistent with the President's proposals for FY2014 through FY2018.[2]

Discretionary spending is provided and controlled through appropriations acts. These acts fund many of the activities commonly associated with federal government functions, such as running executive branch agencies, congressional offices and agencies, and international operations of the government.[3] Thus, the figures showing trends in discretionary budget authority presented below do not reflect the much larger expenditures on program benefits supported by mandatory spending. For some departments, such as Transportation, the division of expenditures into discretionary and mandatory categories can be complex.

Discretionary spending in this report is measured in terms of budget authority. Budget authority for an agency has been compared to having funds in a checking account. Funds are available, subject to congressional restrictions, and can be used to enter into obligations such as contracts or hiring personnel. Outlays occur when the U.S. Treasury disburses funds to honor those obligations. Spending in this report is shown as a percentage of GDP to control for the effects of inflation, population growth, and growth in per capita income. A flat line on such graphs indicates that spending in that category is increasing at the same rate as overall economic growth.

Discussions about the appropriate levels of spending for various policy objectives of the federal government have played an important role in congressional deliberations over funding measures in the last several years and are expected to play a central role as Congress considers decisions affecting the FY2014 budget.[4] As the 113th Congress considers funding levels for FY2014 and beyond, past spending trends may prove useful in framing policy discussions. For example, rapid growth in national defense and other security spending in the past decade has played an important role in fiscal discussions. The sharp increases in federal spending on education, energy, and other areas funded by The American Recovery and Reinvestment Act of 2009 (P.L. 111-5; ARRA) have also played a significant role in recent budget debates.

Discretionary spending caps and budget enforcement mechanisms established in the Budget Control Act of 2011 (P.L. 112-25; BCA) will probably strongly affect the FY2014 budget cycle.[5] The BCA was signed into law on August 2, 2011, after months of intense negotiations over alternative plans to reduce the deficit and raise the debt limit.

---

[1] The President's FY2014 budget was released on April 10, 2013, and is available at http://www.whitehouse.gov/omb/budget/.

[2] The start of the federal fiscal year was changed from July 1 to October 1 in 1976 to accommodate changes in the congressional budget process. The figures omit data for the transition quarter (July 1 to September 30, 1976). It appears that FY2013 data omit the effects related to the March 1, 2013, sequestration triggered by the absence of a Joint Select Committee on Deficit Reduction (Super Committee) plan and final action on FY2013 appropriations. See *FY2014 Budget of the U.S. Government*, Summary Table S-4, note 2.

[3] For a broader analysis of discretionary spending, see CRS Report RL34424, *Trends in Discretionary Spending*, by D. Andrew Austin.

[4] CRS Report R41771, *FY2011 Appropriations in Budgetary Context*, by D. Andrew Austin and Amy Belasco.

[5] CRS Report R41965, *The Budget Control Act of 2011*, by Bill Heniff Jr., Elizabeth Rybicki, and Shannon M. Mahan.

Figures in this report are based on the Office of Management and Budget (OMB) Public Budget Database accompanying the FY2014 budget release.[6] Table 5.1 in the *Historical Tables* volume of the FY2014 budget reports budget authority by function and subfunction, but does not provide a breakdown by discretionary and mandatory subcomponents.[7]

OMB is the official custodian of historical federal budget data. While OMB has attempted to make these data consistent, changes in government accounting standards and agency reorganizations, among other changes, may raise difficulties in comparing data from different fiscal years. For example, the Department of Homeland Security (DHS) was created in 2002 from 22 existing federal agencies or entities.[8] OMB used historical budget data for those agencies or entities to calculate retrospective estimates for DHS.

Budget data in OMB documents may differ from other budget data for various reasons, although differences in historical data are typically small. For example, appropriations budget documents often reflect scorekeeping adjustments. Budget data issued at a later date may include revisions absent from earlier data. In some cases, detailed appropriations data may differ from OMB data, which sometimes do not reflect certain relatively small zero-balance transfers among funds. Differences may also reflect technical differences or different interpretations of federal budget concepts.

Background on Functional Categories

Functional categories provide a means to compare federal funding for activities within broad policy areas that often cut across several federal agencies.[9] Because various federal agencies may have closely related or overlapping responsibilities, and because some agencies have responsibilities in diverse policy areas, budget data divided along functional categories can provide a useful view of federal activities in support of specific national purposes. Superfunction categories, which provide a higher level division of federal activities, are

- National defense,
- Human resources,
- Physical resources, and
- Other functions.

Net interest, Allowances, and Undistributed offsetting receipts could also be considered as separate categories. Superfunction categories for national defense, net interest, allowances, and

---

[6] Data in the OMB Public Budget Database reconcile to information presented in the *Historical Tables* volume of the FY2014 budget. The Public Budget Database itself is available here: http://www.whitehouse.gov/omb/budget/ Supplemental. For a further description and important caveats, see the *Public Budget Database User Guide*, available at http://www.whitehouse.gov/sites/default/files/omb/budget/fy2014/assets/db_guide.pdf.

[7] Table 5.1 of the OMB *Historical Tables* is available at http://www.whitehouse.gov/sites/default/files/omb/budget/ fy2014/assets/hist05z1.xls.

[8] Department of Homeland Security, "Creation of the Department of Homeland Security," available at http://www.dhs.gov/creation-department-homeland-security.

[9] For further background on functional categories, see CRS Report 98-280, *Functional Categories of the Federal Budget*, by Bill Heniff Jr.

---

undistributed offsetting receipts coincide with function categories. Trends in net interest are excluded as federal interest expenditures have been automatically appropriated since 1847. Allowances, which contain items reflecting technical budget adjustments, and undistributed offsetting receipts, are also excluded. Allowances in FY2014 include unspecified cuts to comply with BCA spending caps, future disaster funding costs, and war funding (Overseas Contingency Operations/OCO; Global War on Terror/GWOT) for years after FY2014.[10]

Budget function categories, grouped by superfunctions, are shown in **Table 1**. Subfunction categories provide a finer division of funding levels within narrower policy areas. Subsequent figures follow the ordering of functions in **Table 1**.

---

[10] The allowance for future disaster costs is not included in calculations underlying graphs in order to conform with published data aggregates. Allowances that reflect enforcement of BCA discretionary spending limits are not included, as they are not disaggregated by function.

Table 1. Budget Function Categories by Superfunction

Superfunction	Code	Function / Subfunction
National Defense		
	50	**National defense**
	51	Dept. of Defense-Military
	53	Atomic energy defense activities
	54	Defense-related activities
Human Resources		
	500	**Education, training, employment, and social services**
	501	Elementary, secondary, and vocational education
	502	Higher education
	503	Research and general education aids
	504	Training and employment
	505	Other labor services
	506	Social services
	550	**Health**
	551	Health care services
	552	Health research and training
	554	Consumer and occupational health and safety
	570	**Medicare**
	571	Medicare
	600	**Income security**
	601	Gen. retirement & disability insurance (exc. Soc. Sec.)
	602	Federal employee retirement and disability
	603	Unemployment compensation
	604	Housing assistance
	605	Food and nutrition assistance
	609	Other income security
	650	**Social security**
	651	Social security
	700	**Veterans benefits and services**
	701	Income security for veterans
	702	Veterans education, training, & rehabilitation
	703	Hospital and medical care for veterans
	704	Veterans housing
	705	Other veterans benefits and services
Physical Resources		
	270	**Energy**
	271	Energy supply
	272	Energy conservation
	274	Emergency energy preparedness
	276	Energy information, policy, and regulation
	300	**Natural resources and environment**
	301	Water resources
	302	Conservation and land management
	303	Recreational resources
	304	Pollution control and abatement
	306	Other natural resources

Superfunction	Code	Function / Subfunction
	370	**Commerce and housing credit**
	371	Mortgage credit
	372	Postal service
	373	Deposit insurance
	376	Other advancement of commerce
	400	**Transportation**
	401	Ground transportation
	402	Air transportation
	403	Water transportation
	407	Other transportation
	450	**Community and regional development**
	451	Community development
	452	Area and regional development
	453	Disaster relief and insurance
Other Functions		
	150	**International affairs**
	151	Intl. dev. and humanitarian assistance
	152	Intl. security assistance
	153	Conduct of foreign affairs
	154	Foreign information & exchange activities
	155	Intl. financial programs
	250	**General science, space, and technology**
	251	General science and basic research
	252	Space flight, research & supporting activities
	350	**Agriculture**
	351	Farm income stabilization
	352	Agricultural research and services
	750	**Administration of justice**
	751	Federal law enforcement activities
	752	Federal litigative and judicial activities
	753	Federal correctional activities
	754	Criminal justice assistance
	800	**General government**
	801	Legislative functions
	802	Executive direction and mgmt.
	803	Central fiscal operations
	804	General property and records mgmt.
	805	Central personnel mgmt.
	806	General purpose fiscal assistance
	808	Other general government
	809	Deductions for offsetting receipts
Net Interest		
	900	**Net interest**
	901	Interest on Treasury debt securities (gross)
	902	Interest received by on-budget trust funds
	903	Interest received by off-budget trust funds
	908	Other interest

Superfunction	Code	Function / Subfunction
	909	Other Investment and income
Allowances		
	920	**Allowances**
	921	Adjustment for BCA Cap on Security Spending
	924	Adjustment for BCA Cap on Non-Security Spending
	925	Future Disaster Costs
	929	Plug for Outyear War Costs
Undistributed Offsetting Receipts		
	950	**Undistributed offsetting receipts**
	951	Employer share, employee retirement (on-budget)
	952	Employer share, employee retirement (off-budget)
	953	Rents & royalties on the Outer Continental Shelf
	954	Sale of major assets
	959	Other undistributed offsetting receipts

Source: CRS, based on OMB data.

Note: Allowances subfunctions often change from one year to the next.

Discretionary Spending in the FY2014 Budget

The BCA, absent further modification by Congress, will likely frame budget discussions for FY2014. Spending limitations on discretionary spending are slated to make sharp reductions in defense and non-defense spending in FY2013 and FY2014.[11]

When the Joint Select Committee on Deficit Reduction (JSC), known as the "Super Committee," did not present a plan to achieve at least $1.2 trillion in deficit reduction over FY2013-FY2021, the original BCA caps were then superseded by *revised caps*, which imposed separate limits on base defense (budget function 050) and non-defense spending. Base defense funding covers normal costs of national defense, while war costs are not subject to BCA caps.[12] The sum of total discretionary spending under the original and revised caps was the same. Further reductions of $109 billion for each year from the revised cap levels, split between defense and non-defense, were slated to occur in each year from FY2013 through FY2021. In FY2013 savings were to be made through sequestration, and in years FY2014-FY2021 savings are slated to occur through a lowering of the discretionary spending caps. Those lowered caps, along with interest savings and an ongoing sequester of non-exempt mandatory spending, were designed to capture the $1.2 trillion in budget savings in the absence of a Super Committee plan.

The American Taxpayer Relief Act (H.R. 8; P.L. 112-240; ATRA) delayed the Super Committee sequester by two months, from January 2, 2013, to March 1, 2013.[13] In addition, the size of the

---

[11] For a more complete description of recent budget legislation, see CRS Report RL34424, *Trends in Discretionary Spending*, by D. Andrew Austin.

[12] War costs, however, are not exempt from sequestration. Those costs are described as Overseas Contingency Operations (OCO) in budget documents.

[13] For details, see CRS Report R42949, *The American Taxpayer Relief Act of 2012: Modifications to the Budget Enforcement Procedures in the Budget Control Act*, by Bill Heniff Jr.

FY2013 sequestration cuts were reduced from $109 billion to $85 billion.[14] Discretionary caps on FY2014 defense and non-defense funding, as part of an offset for that reduction, were reduced by $4 billion each. Thus, the revised cap on FY2014 defense funding was reduced from $556 billion to $552 billion. The revised cap on FY2014 non-defense funding was reduced from $510 billion to $506 billion. Defense and non-defense spending are slated for reductions of $54.7 billion each, allocated between discretionary and mandatory spending. Because non-exempt defense mandatory spending is relatively small, most of the defense reduction would be borne by base defense discretionary via a lowered cap. According to preliminary OMB estimates, the lowered FY2014 cap for base defense discretionary BA will be $468.8 billion.[15]

On the non-defense side for FY2014, Medicare patient care expenses and other non-exempt mandatory spending would bear $17.5 billion of the $54.7 billion reduction through a sequester, according to OMB estimates.[16] The remaining $37.2 billion would be borne by non-defense discretionary spending via a lowering of its revised cap ($506 billion) to $468.8 billion.

For FY2013 Super Committee sequester, the March 1, 2013, Medicare mandatory patient care spending was reduced by $11.3 billion, other non-defense mandatory spending by $5.4 billion, and non-defense discretionary BA was reduced by $25.8 billion.[17] The reduction slated for non-defense in FY2014 will be larger than FY2013 for two reasons. First, non-defense sequester was half of $85 billion, rather than the half of $109 billion sequester slated for FY2014. Second, the reduction of Medicare patient care spending is limited to 2%, which implies that increases in the size of non-defense reductions will be chiefly borne by discretionary programs.

The Administration has proposed lowering of BCA caps on discretionary spending, which would yield about $800 billion over the FY2013-FY2021 period with discretionary spending cap reductions of $202 billion that would start to take effect in FY2017.[18] Thus, projected discretionary spending for FY2014-FY2018 shown in the figures below, which presume the President's budgetary proposals are adopted, reflect an assumption that BCA constraints on discretionary spending will be loosened.

Discretionary spending as a share of GDP, if BCA caps remain in place, will decline to levels well below that seen in recent decades. In real dollar terms (i.e., adjusting for inflation but not for growth in population or the economy), discretionary base defense spending would revert to a level slightly above its FY2007 level, while non-defense discretionary spending would revert a level near its 2002 level.[19] In later years, BCA caps would allow for modest growth in nominal

---

[14] Thus the size of the FY2013 sequester was reduced by $24 billion.

[15] OMB, Sequestration Preview Report to the President and Congress for FY2014, Table 1, available at http://www.whitehouse.gov/sites/default/files/omb/assets/legislative_reports/ fy14_preview_and_joint_committee_reductions_reports_04102013.pdf.

[16] Ibid., Table 3, p. 15.

[17] The BCA specifies sequester reductions in mandatory spending in terms of outlays. For discretionary spending, the Super Committee sequester canceled budget authority for FY2013. Discretionary spending reductions are slated to be implemented through lowered caps on budget authority from FY2014 through FY2021. See OMB, *Report to the Congress on the Joint Committee Sequestration for Fiscal Year 2013*, March 1, 2013; available at http://www.whitehouse.gov/sites/default/files/omb/assets/legislative_reports/fy13ombjcsequestrationreport.pdf.

[18] OMB, *FY2014 Budget of the U.S. Government*, p. 45. See Table 6 of memorandum cited below for $800 billion estimate for difference between BCA revised caps and lowered caps.

[19] For details, see Congressional Research Service, "The Budget Control Act and Alternate Defense and Non-Defense Spending Paths, FY2012-FY2021," by Amy Belasco and Andrew Austin, November 16, 2012, available from authors. This comparison is made in terms of budget authority. Before passage of ATRA, BCA provisions were slated to bring (continued...)

(i.e., not adjusted for inflation) terms. By contrast, mandatory spending and net interest costs are projected to rise, implying that discretionary spending's share of total federal spending would continue to fall.

Actual discretionary budget authority totals will differ from BCA discretionary caps because some types of spending are not subject to caps, such as war spending, certain amounts of disaster relief assistance, and program integrity initiatives. In addition, scorekeeping adjustments typically lead to differences between scored totals of budget authority used to check conformity to BCA spending limits and other budget totals that do not include those adjustments.

Negative Budget Authority

Within the federal budget concepts, certain inflows, such as offsetting receipts, offsetting collections, some user fees, and "profits" from federal loan programs, are treated as negative budget authority.[20] The federal government uses a modified form of accrual accounting for loan and loan guarantee programs since passage of the Federal Credit Reform Act (FCRA) as well as for certain federal retirement programs.[21] OMB calculates net subsidy rates according to FCRA rules for loan and loan guarantee programs. In some cases, FCRA calculations yield negative net subsidy levels, implying that the federal government appears to make a profit on those loans.[22] FCRA subsidy calculations, however, omit risk adjustments.[23] The true economic cost of federal credit guarantees can be substantially underestimated when risk adjustments are omitted.[24]

Historical Spending Trends

Federal spending trends in functional areas are affected by changing assessments of national priorities, evolving international challenges, and economic conditions, as well as changing social characteristics and demographics of the U.S. population. Some of the trends and events that have had dramatic effects on federal spending are outlined below. Other CRS products provide background on more specific policy areas.

(...continued)

discretionary base defense spending to its FY2007 level and non-defense spending to near its level in FY2003 or FY2004. Inflation adjustments made using GDP price index.

[20] See OMB, FY2014 Budget, *Analytic Perspectives*, ch. 11, "Budget Concepts." In particular, pp. 117-122 cover these topics.

[21] CRS Report RL30346, *Federal Credit Reform: Implementation of the Changed Budgetary Treatment of Direct Loans and Loan Guarantees*, by James M. Bickley, available upon request.

[22] For example, some Federal Housing Administration mortgage programs and some federal student loan programs have been estimated to yield negative net subsidies.

[23] While the FCRA calculations include estimates of default costs, they do not discount more volatile income flows, as a private firm would.

[24] U.S. Congressional Budget Office, *Estimating the Value of Subsidies for Federal Loans and Loan Guarantees*, August 2004, available at http://cbo.gov/doc.cfm?index=5751. CBO and OMB include risk adjustments in estimates of the costs associated with the TARP as mandated by the Emergency Economic Stabilization Act of 2008 (P.L. 110-343; EESA). See U.S. Congressional Budget Office, *The Budget and Economic Outlook: Fiscal Years 2009 to 2019*, January 7, 2009, pp. 25-26, available at http://www.cbo.gov/ftpdocs/99xx/doc9957/01-07-Outlook.pdf; Testimony of Elizabeth Warren, Chair of the Congressional Oversight Panel, in Congress, Senate Banking Committee, *Pulling Back the TARP: Oversight of the Financial Rescue Program*, hearings, 111th Congress, 1st sess., February 5, 2009, available at http://banking.senate.gov/public/_files/Warrentestimonyfinal2509.pdf.

Cold War, Peace Dividend, and the Global War on Terror

The allocation of discretionary spending between defense and non-defense programs is one reflection of changing federal priorities over time. **Figure 1** shows defense and non-defense discretionary funding as a percentage of GDP. **Figure 2** shows subfunctions within the National Defense (050) budget function. The Department of Defense (DOD)-Military subfunction accounts for over 95% of funding within that budget function.

Figure 1. Discretionary Defense and Non-Defense Spending, FY1976-FY2018

Budget authority as a percentage of GDP

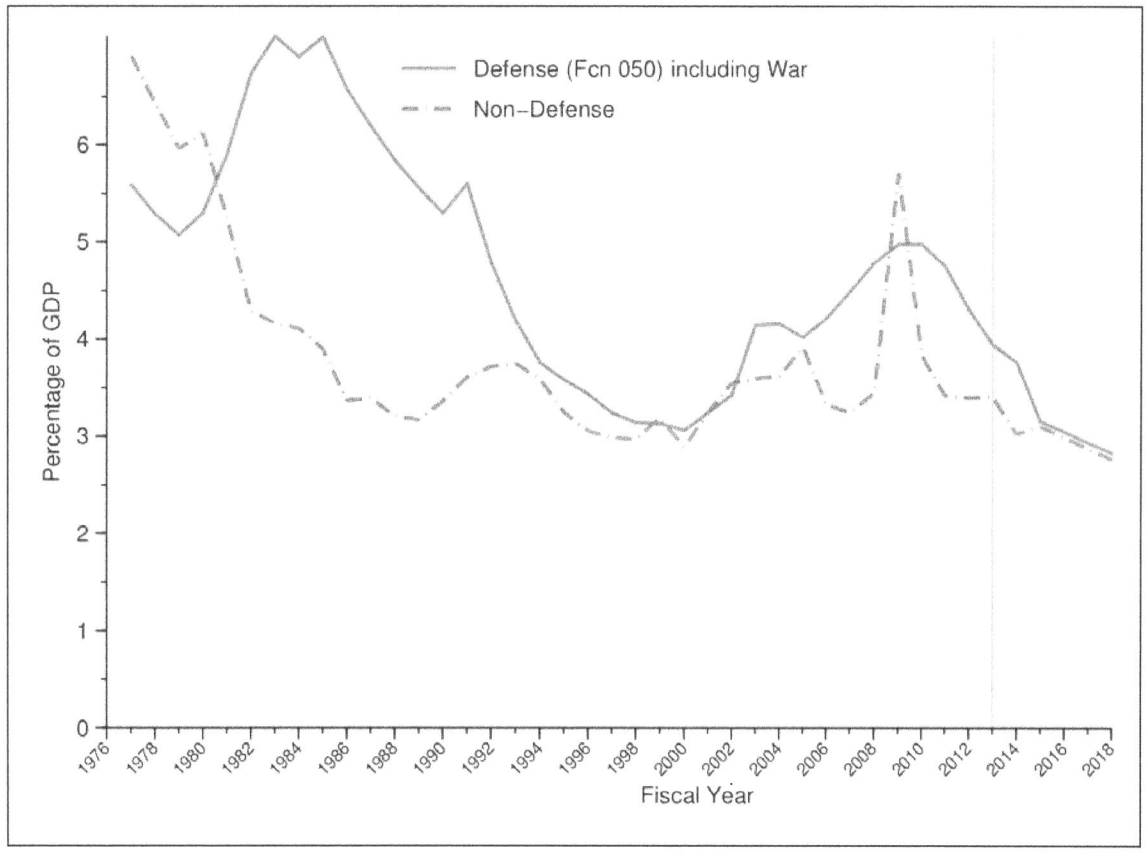

Source: CRS analysis of OMB data.

Notes: Defense is defined as funding for the National Defense (050) budget function; non-defense is the remainder. FY1976-FY2012 are historical data; FY2013 is estimated; FY2014-FY2018 reflect the President's FY2014 budget proposals. This figure assumes unspecified cuts to meet BCA caps are borne by non-defense programs. See text for other important caveats.

Relations between the United States and its allies on one hand, and the Union of Soviet Socialist Republics (USSR) and its allies on the other were the dominant security concern in the half century following the Second World War. In the early 1970s, U.S. involvement in the Vietnam War wound down, while the United States and the USSR moved towards detente, permitting a thaw in Cold War relations between the two superpowers and a reduction in defense spending relative to the size of the economy.[25]

Figure 2. National Defense (050) Subfunctions

Discretionary budget authority as a percentage of GDP, FY1976-FY2018

Source: CRS, based on OMB data from the FY2014 budget submission

Notes: FY2014-FY2018 levels reflect Administration proposals and projections. See OMB budget documents for further caveats.

Following intervention by the USSR in Afghanistan in 1979, military spending increased sharply.[26] Defense spending continued to increase until 1986, as concern shifted to domestic priorities and the need to reduce large budget deficits. The collapse in 1989 of most of the Warsaw Pact governments in Central and Eastern Europe and the 1990-1991 disintegration of the Soviet Union was followed by a reduction in federal defense spending, allowing a "peace dividend" that relaxed fiscal pressures. [27]

---

[25] For a history of deficit finance and American wars, see Robert D. Hormats, *The Price of Liberty*, (New York: Times Books, 2007). Also see CRS Report RL31176, *Financing Issues and Economic Effects of American Wars*, by Marc Labonte and Mindy R. Levit.

[26] For one view of budgetary politics in the early 1980s, see David Stockman, *The Triumph of Politics*, (New York: Harper & Row, 1986).

[27] The Warsaw Treaty Organization, established in 1955, included Albania, Bulgaria, Czechoslovakia, the German Democratic Republic, Hungary, Poland, Romania, and the Soviet Union.

The attacks on the World Trade Center towers in New York City and on the Pentagon on September 11, 2001, were followed by sharp increases in homeland security spending. Defense spending also increased dramatically with the start of the Afghanistan war in October 2001 and the Iraq war in March 2003.[28] U.S. combat troops were withdrawn from Iraq in December 2011, and President Obama has announced that most U.S. troops would be withdrawn from Afghanistan by the end of 2014.[29]

Spending on non-defense security spending also rose after the attacks of September 11, 2001, as the federal government overhauled airport security procedures, and then established the Department of Homeland Security. In 2005, hurricanes Katrina and Rita led to a spike in disaster relief spending.[30] Non-security spending also rose to fund new initiatives in education and in other areas.[31]

In 2007, a severe credit crunch affected global financial markets, which led to a fully fledged financial crisis in 2008 and a severe economic recession. The American Recovery and Reinvestment Act of 2009 (P.L. 111-5; ARRA), designed to stimulate the economy and prevent further slowing of economic activity, sharply increased federal spending on education, energy, and support for state and local governments. ARRA also included broad tax cuts through a Making Work Pay credit and other provisions. The decline in federal revenues and the increase in spending caused the deficit to treble from $459 billion in FY2008 to $1.4 trillion in FY2009.

Since FY2010, base defense discretionary spending has been held flat and non-defense discretionary spending has been reduced significantly.[32] The BCA, as noted above, reimposed discretionary spending limits that are slated to remain in place until FY2021.

The Recovery Act

After the financial crisis of 2007-2008 plunged the United States in the deepest economic recession in decades, Congress passed the American Recovery and Reinvestment Act of 2009 (P.L. 111-5; ARRA), often known as the Recovery Act. ARRA includes support for state and local governments in the form of increased infrastructure, Medicaid, school funding, funding for health care IT, extended unemployment benefits, as well as tax cuts and rebates among other provisions.[33] According to initial CBO estimates, ARRA provisions were expected to total $787.2

---

[28] CRS Report RL33110, *The Cost of Iraq, Afghanistan, and Other Global War on Terror Operations Since 9/11*, by Amy Belasco. The Afghan and Iraq wars, along with other related activities, are often called the Global War on Terror (GWOT).

[29] See CRS Report RL30588, *Afghanistan: Post-Taliban Governance, Security, and U.S. Policy*, by Kenneth Katzman.

[30] See CRS Report R40708, *Disaster Relief Funding and Emergency Supplemental Appropriations*, by Bruce R. Lindsay and Justin Murray.

[31] The Obama Administration defined security spending in its FY2012 budget as funding for Department of Defense-Military (subfunction 051); the Department of Energy's National Nuclear Security Administration; International Affairs (function 150, which includes State Department and related agencies); the Department of Homeland Security; and the Department of Veterans Affairs. The BCA defined security similarly, except that it included all military activities within the Department of Defense excluding war funding (i.e., defined by department rather than by subfunction), and also included the Intelligence Community Management Account.

[32] The base defense budget excludes war funding (Overseas Contingency Operations).

[33] For more information on the provisions of ARRA, see CRS Report R40537, *American Recovery and Reinvestment Act of 2009 (P.L. 111-5): Summary and Legislative History*, by Clinton T. Brass et al.

billion in increased spending and reduced taxes over the FY2009-FY2019 period or just over 5% of GDP in 2008, while a more recent CBO estimate put the total at $814 billion.[34]

The effects of Recovery Act spending can be seen in **Figure 3**, where pronounced increases in education, training, employment, and social services subfunctions can be seen for FY2009. Smaller increases can be seen in **Figure 9**, which shows energy subfunctions, and in **Figure 10**, which shows natural resources and environment subfunctions.

Figure 3. Education, Training, Employment, and Social Services (500) Subfunctions

Discretionary budget authority as a percentage of GDP, FY1976-FY2018

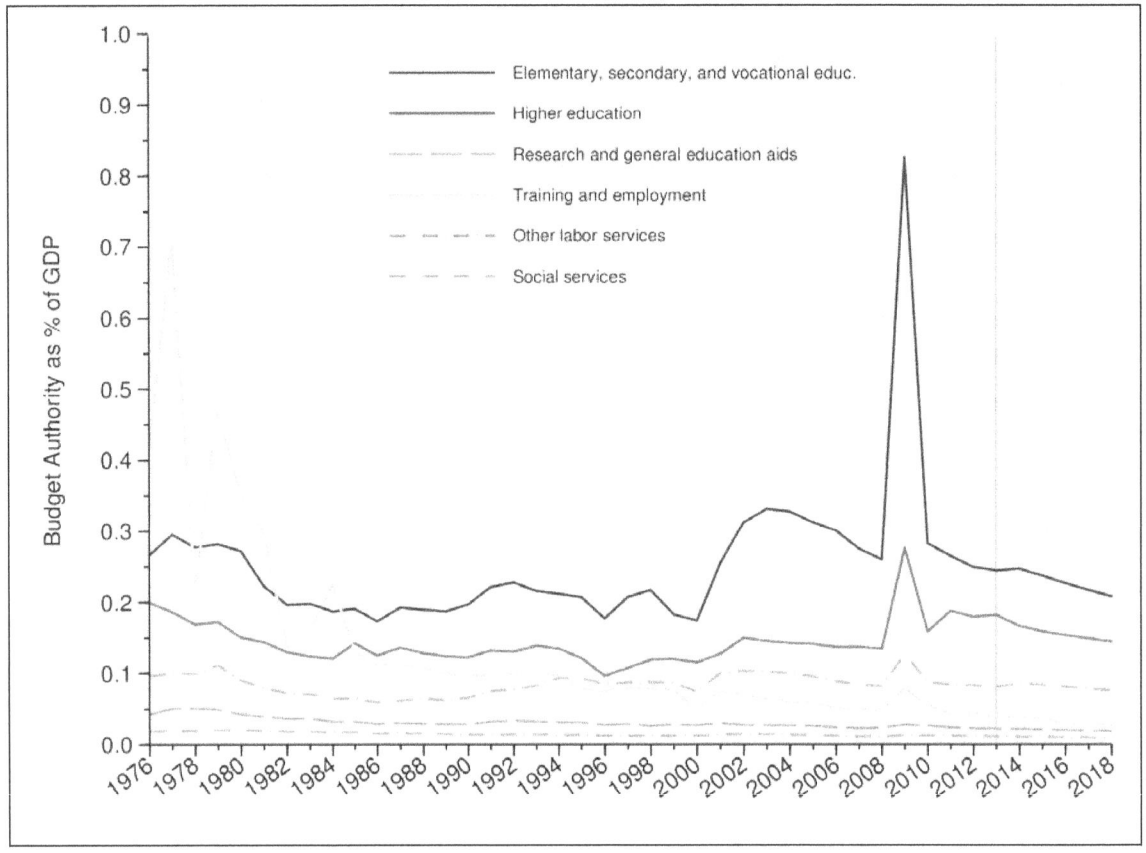

Source: CRS, based on OMB data from the FY2014 budget submission.

Notes: FY2014-FY2018 levels reflect Administration proposals and projections. See OMB budget documents for further caveats.

Federal Health Programs

Costs of federal health programs continue to play a central role in budgetary discussions. The costs of the largest federal health programs, Medicare and the federal portion of Medicaid costs,

---

[34] For initial estimates, see U.S. Congressional Budget Office, *Cost Estimate For the Conference Agreement For H.R. 1*, February 13, 2009, available at http://cbo.gov/ftpdocs/99xx/doc9989/hr1conference.pdf. For a later assessment, see CBO, *Budget and Economic Outlook: An Update*, August 2010, Box 1-2, available at http://www.cbo.gov/ftpdocs/117xx/doc11705/08-18-Update.pdf.

are nearly all mandatory. Administrative costs, which account for a small portion of those costs, are nearly all funded as discretionary spending. Federal health research and veterans' health care is mostly funded through discretionary spending, as are certain public health clinics. Trends in funding of health subfunctions are shown in two separate figures. Larger programs (health care services/subfunction 551 and Medicare/function 570/subfunction 571) are shown in **Figure 4**, and smaller programs (health research and training/subfunction 552 and consumer and occupational health and safety/subfunction 554) are shown in **Figure 5**. The National Institutes of Health (NIH) are the largest part of the health research and training subfunction. Veterans' health programs, which fall under the veterans benefits and services function, are also shown in **Figure 8** to make comparisons among those programs easier.

Figure 4. Health Care Services (Subfunction 551) and Medicare (Subfunction 571)

Discretionary budget authority as a percentage of GDP, FY1976-FY2018

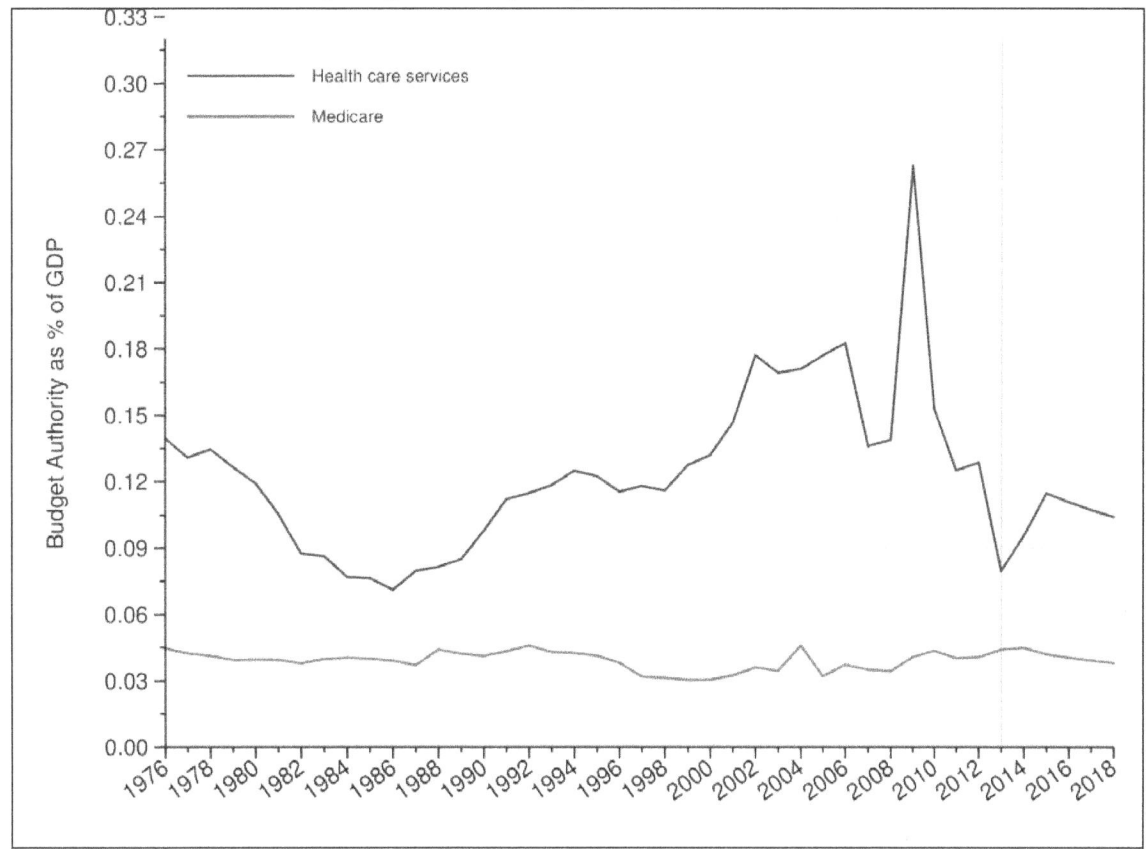

Source: CRS, based on OMB data from the FY2014 budget submission.

Notes: FY2014-FY2018 levels reflect Administration proposals and projections. Discretionary BA for Medicare funds program administration, and does not generally fund program benefits. See OMB budget documents for further caveats.

Figure 5. Smaller Health Subfunctions

Discretionary budget authority as a percentage of GDP, FY1976-FY2018

Source: CRS, based on OMB data from the FY2014 budget submission.

Notes: Hospital and medical care for veterans (703) presented here for comparison and also appears in **Figure 9**. FY2014-FY2018 levels reflect Administration proposals and projections. See OMB budget documents for further caveats.

Figure 6. Income Security (600) Subfunctions

Discretionary budget authority as a percentage of GDP, FY1976-FY2018

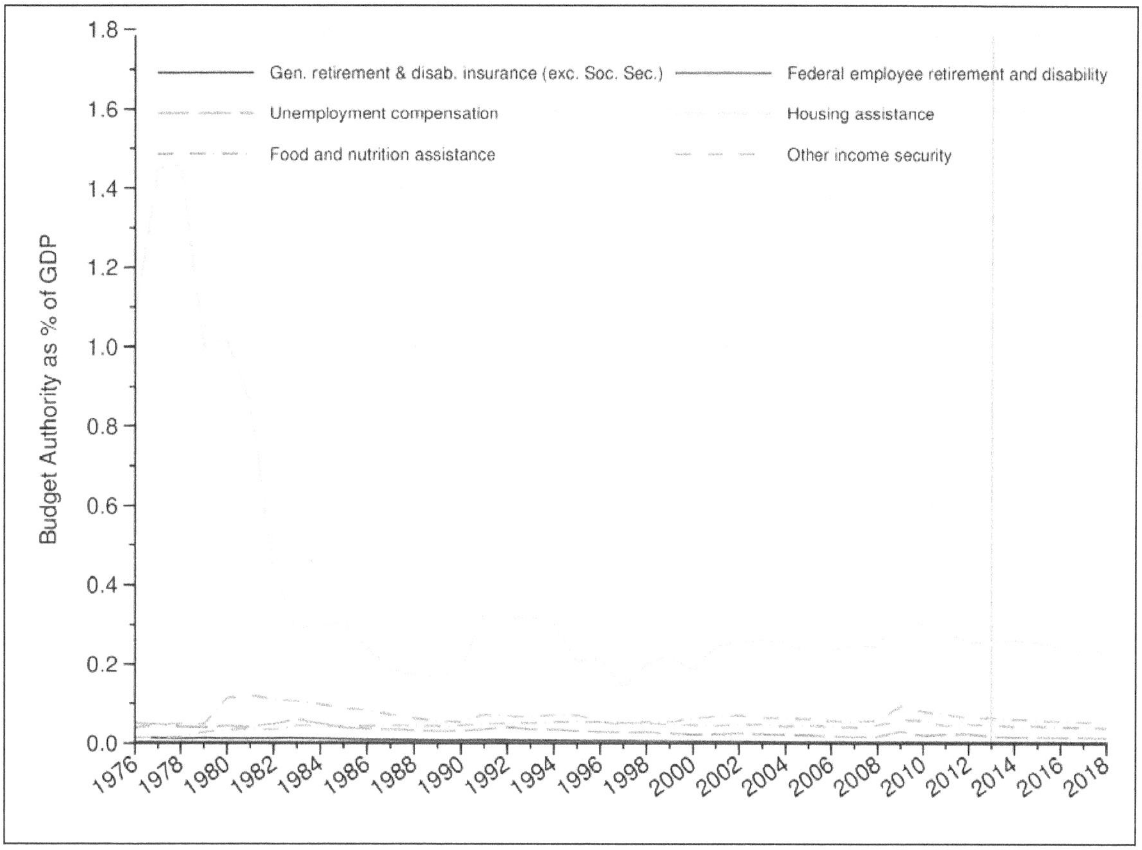

Source: CRS, based on OMB data from the FY2014 budget submission.

Notes: Discretionary funding for income security programs supports program administration; most income security benefits are generally funded by mandatory spending, which is not shown here. FY2014-FY2018 levels reflect Administration proposals and projections. See OMB budget documents for further caveats.

Figure 7. Social Security (650) Subfunction

Discretionary budget authority as a percentage of GDP, FY1976-FY2018

Source: CRS, based on OMB data from the FY2014 budget submission.

Notes: Discretionary funding for Social Security supports program administration; Social Security benefits are generally funded by mandatory spending, which is not shown here. FY2014-FY2018 levels reflect Administration proposals and projections. See OMB budget documents for further caveats.

Figure 8. Veterans Benefits and Services (700) Subfunctions

Discretionary budget authority as a percentage of GDP, FY1976-FY2018

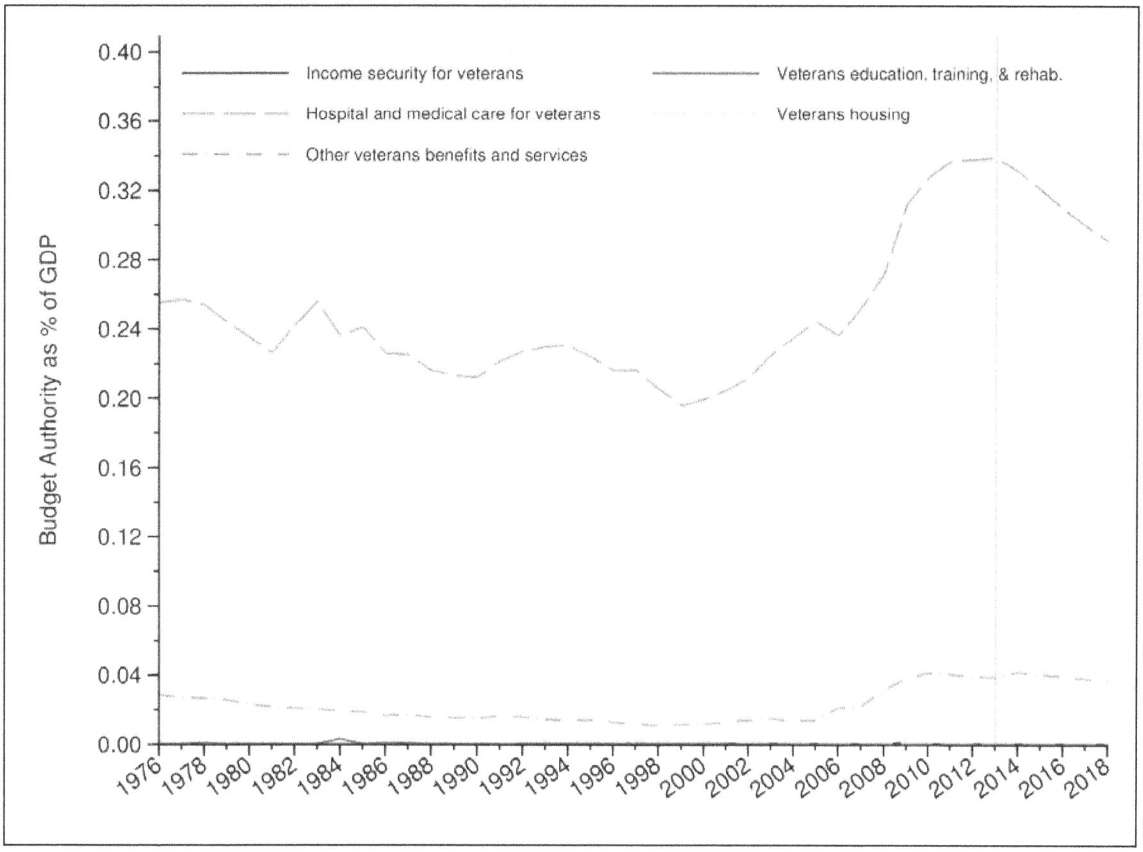

Source: CRS, based on OMB data from the FY2014 budget submission.

Notes: FY2014-FY2018 levels reflect Administration proposals and projections. See OMB budget documents for further caveats. Note that mandatory Veterans Affairs expenditures, which chiefly support income security programs, are not reflected here.

Figure 9. Energy (270) Subfunctions

Discretionary budget authority as a percentage of GDP, FY1976-FY2018

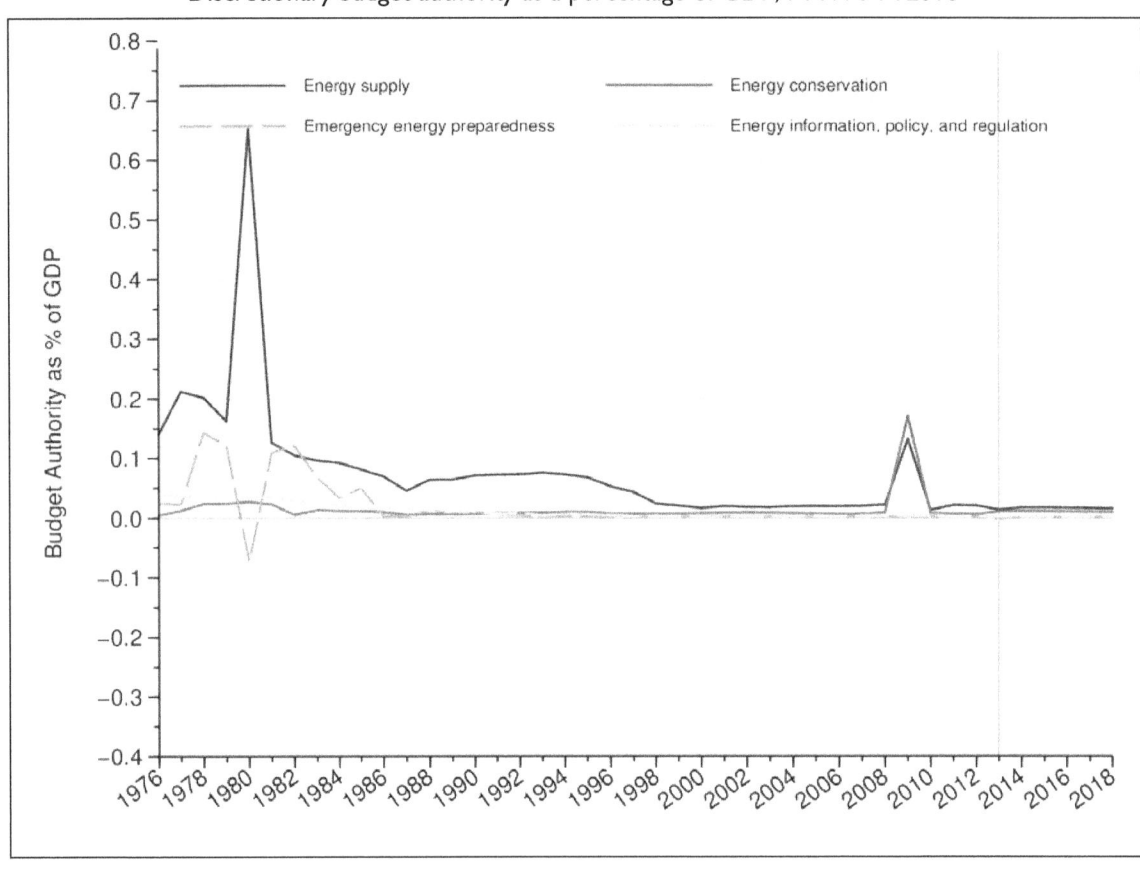

Source: CRS, based on OMB data from FY2014 budget submission.

Notes: FY2014-FY2018 levels reflect Administration proposals and projections. See OMB budget documents for further caveats.

Figure 10. Natural Resources and Environment (300) Subfunctions

Discretionary budget authority as a percentage of GDP, FY1976-FY2018

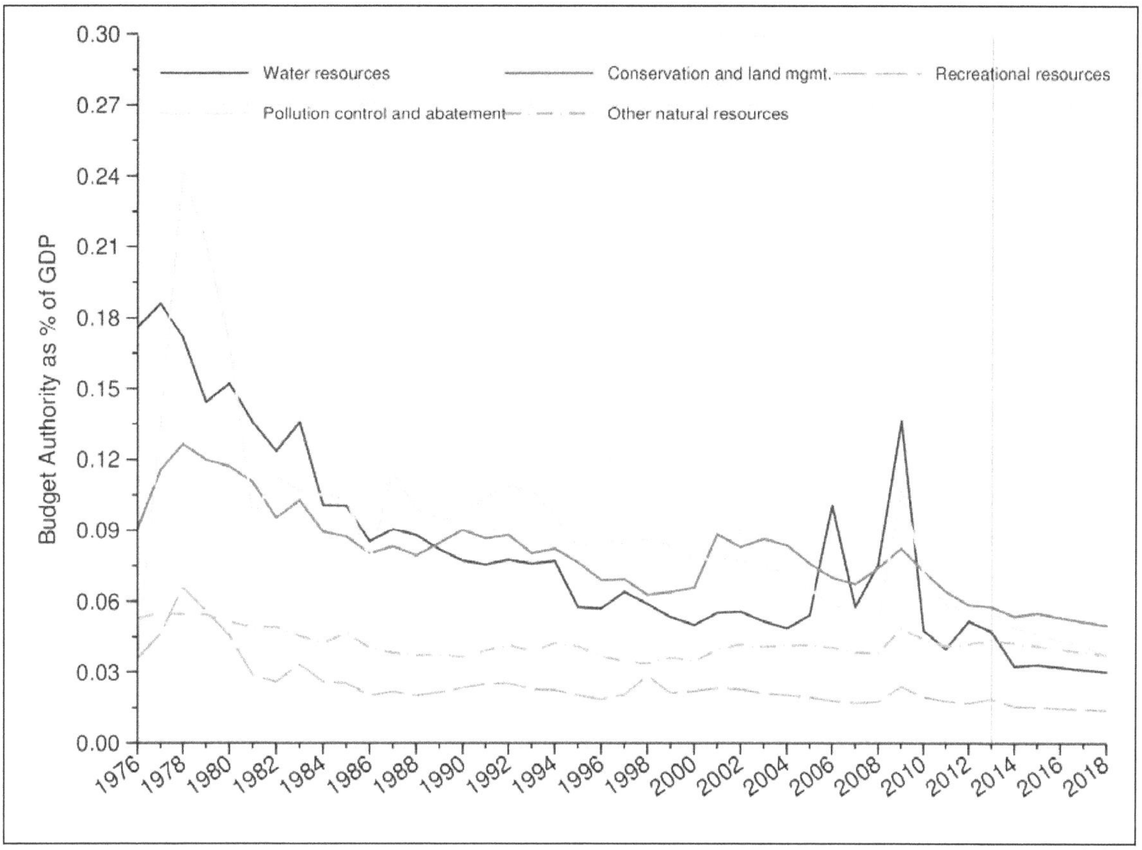

Source: CRS, based on OMB data from FY2014 budget submission.

Notes: FY2014-FY2018 levels reflect Administration proposals and projections. See OMB budget documents for further caveats.

Figure 11. Commerce and Housing Credit Subfunctions

Discretionary budget authority as a percentage of GDP, FY1976-FY2018

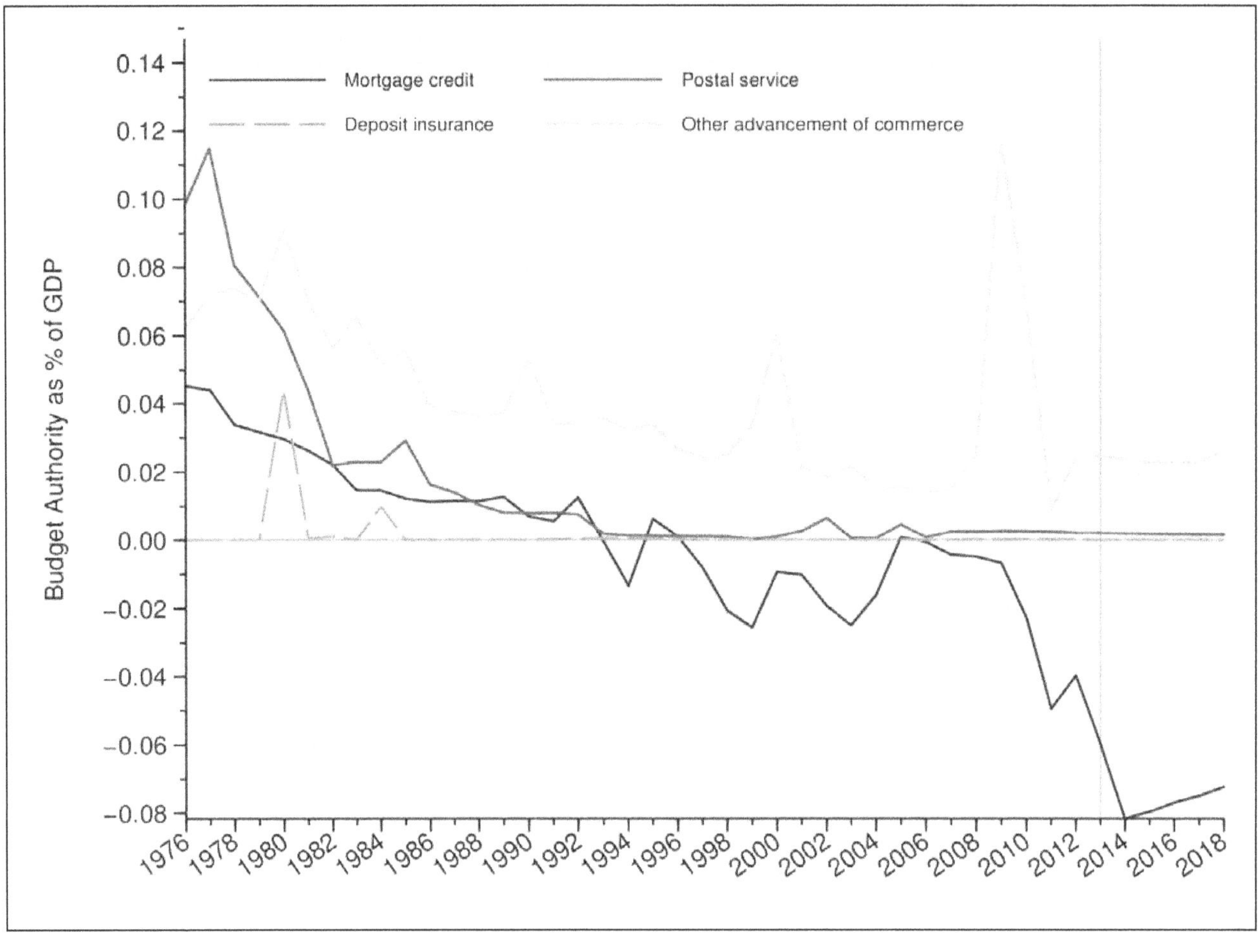

Source: CRS, based on OMB data from FY2014 budget submission.

Notes: FY2014-FY2018 levels reflect Administration proposals and projections. See OMB budget documents for further caveats.

Figure 12. Transportation (400) Subfunctions

Discretionary budget authority as a percentage of GDP, FY1976-FY2018

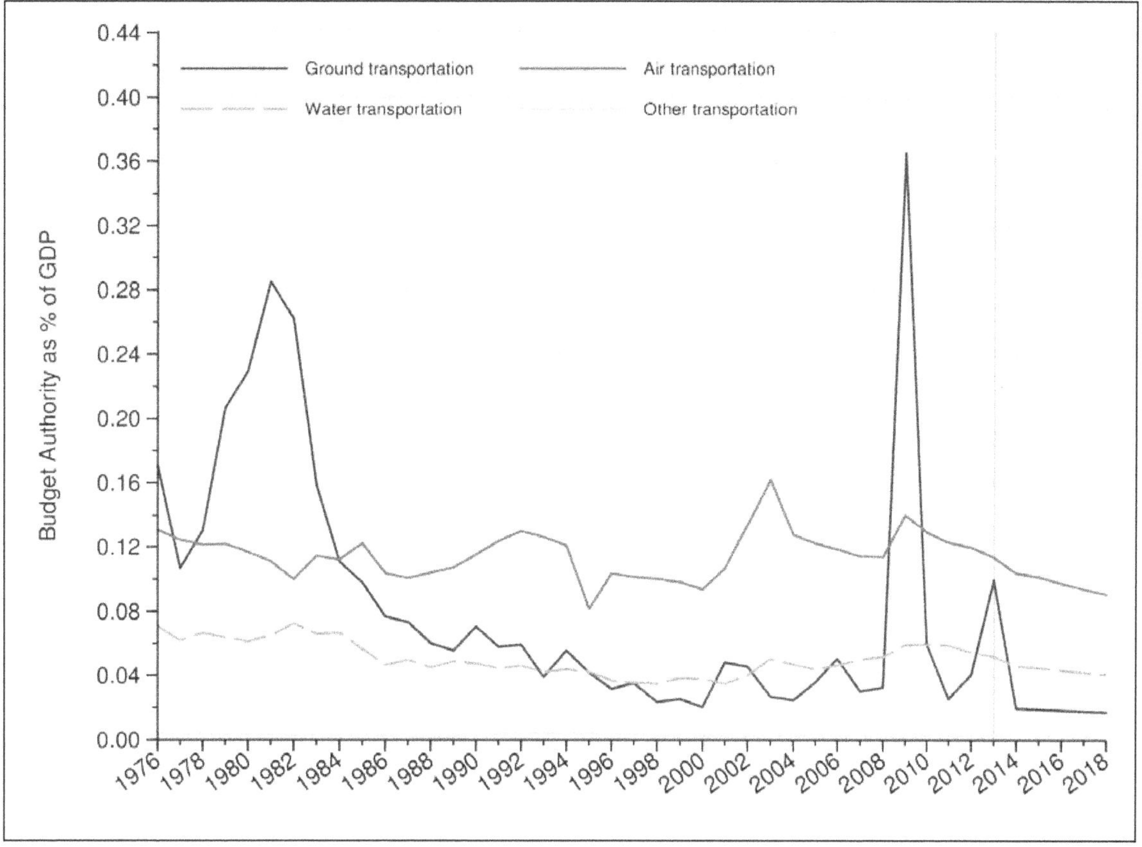

Source: CRS, based on OMB data from FY2014 budget submission.

Notes: FY2014-FY2018 levels reflect Administration proposals and projections. See OMB budget documents for further caveats.

Figure 13. Community and Regional Development (450) Subfunctions

Discretionary budget authority as a percentage of GDP, FY1976-FY2018

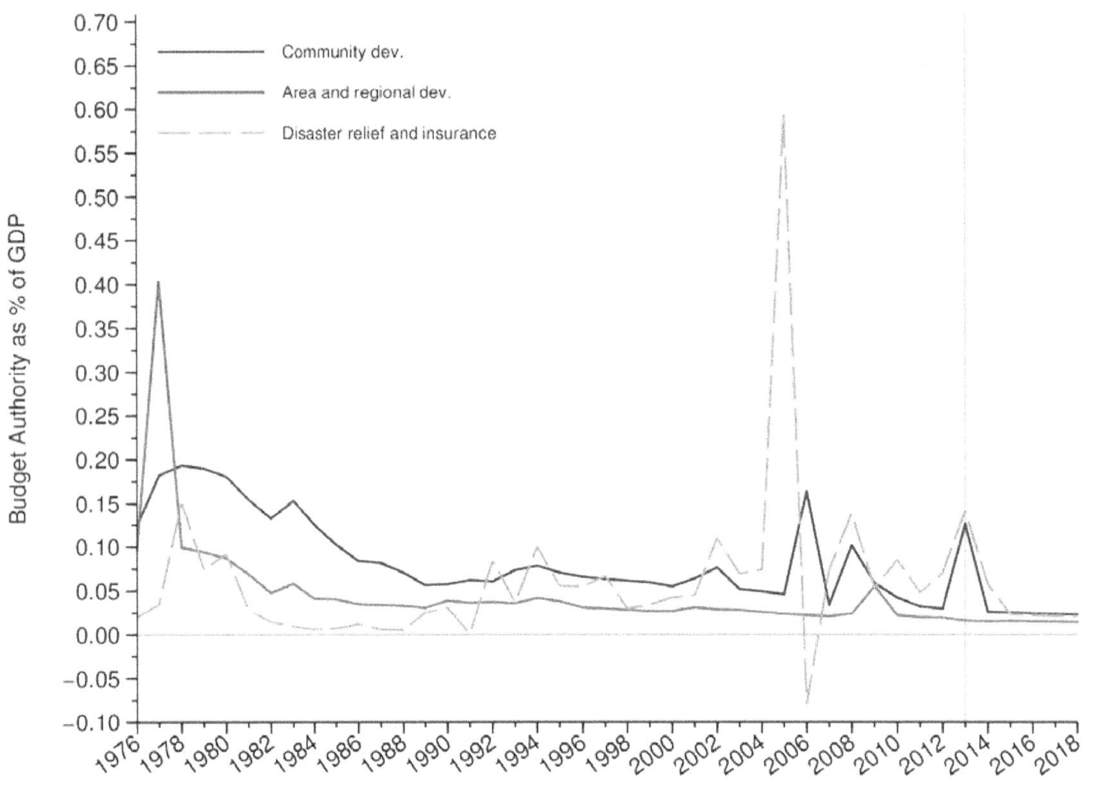

Source: CRS, based on OMB data from FY2014 budget submission.

Notes: FY2014-FY2018 levels reflect Administration proposals and projections. See OMB budget documents for further caveats.

Figure 14. International Affairs (150) Subfunctions

Discretionary budget authority as a percentage of GDP, FY1976-FY2018

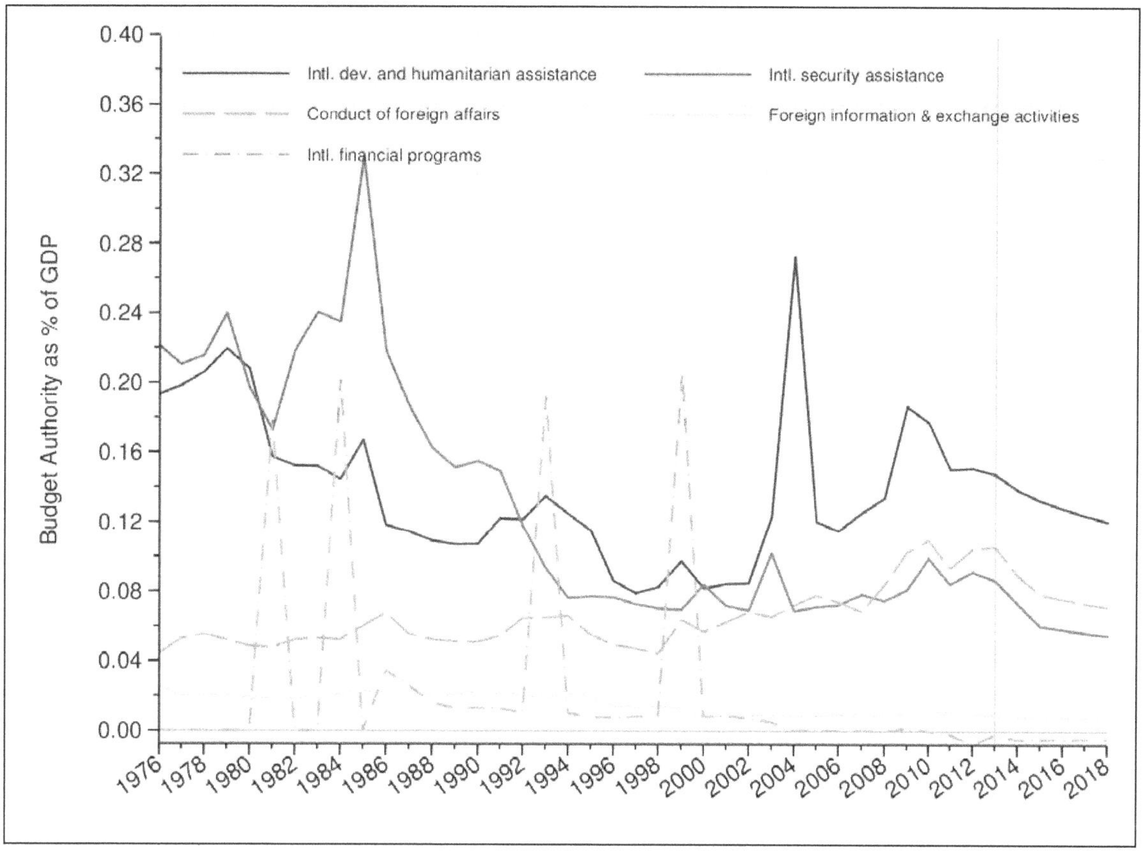

Source: CRS, based on OMB data from FY2014 budget submission.

Notes: FY2014-FY2018 levels reflect Administration proposals and projections. See OMB budget documents for further caveats.

Figure 15. General Science, Space, and Technology (250) Subfunctions

Discretionary budget authority as a percentage of GDP, FY1976-FY2018

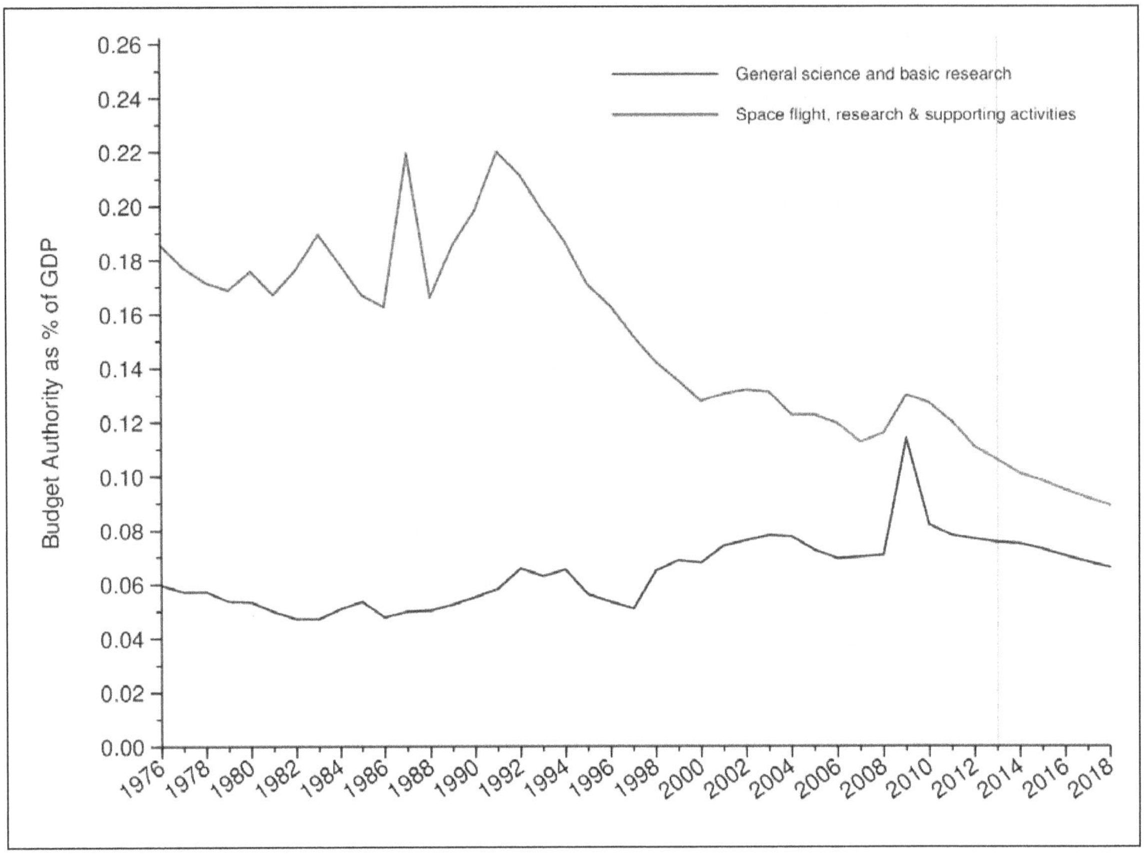

Source: CRS, based on OMB data from FY2014 budget submission.

Notes: FY2014-FY2018 levels reflect Administration proposals and projections. See OMB budget documents for further caveats.

Figure 16. Agriculture (350) Subfunctions

Discretionary budget authority as a percentage of GDP, FY1976-FY2018

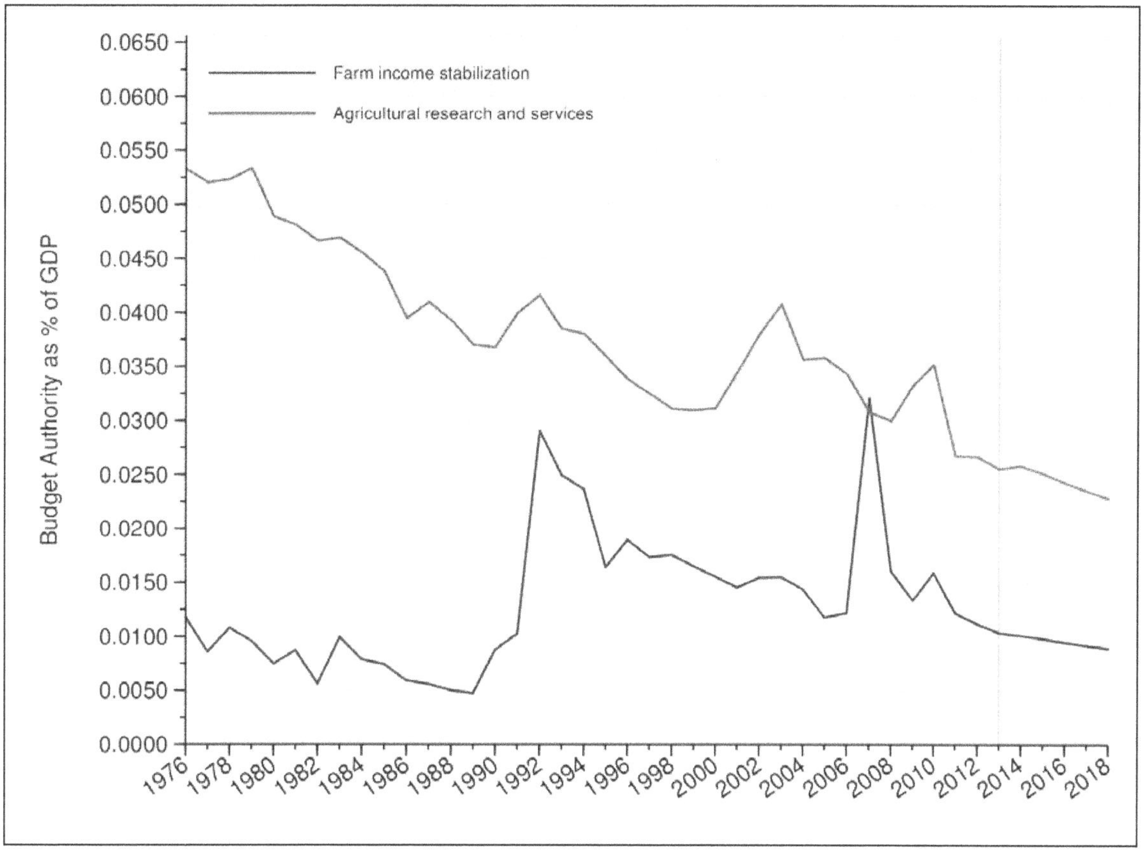

Source: CRS, based on OMB data from FY2014 budget submission.

Notes: FY2014-FY2018 levels reflect Administration proposals and projections. See OMB budget documents for further caveats.

Figure 17. Administration of Justice (750) Subfunctions

Discretionary budget authority as a percentage of GDP, FY1976-FY2018

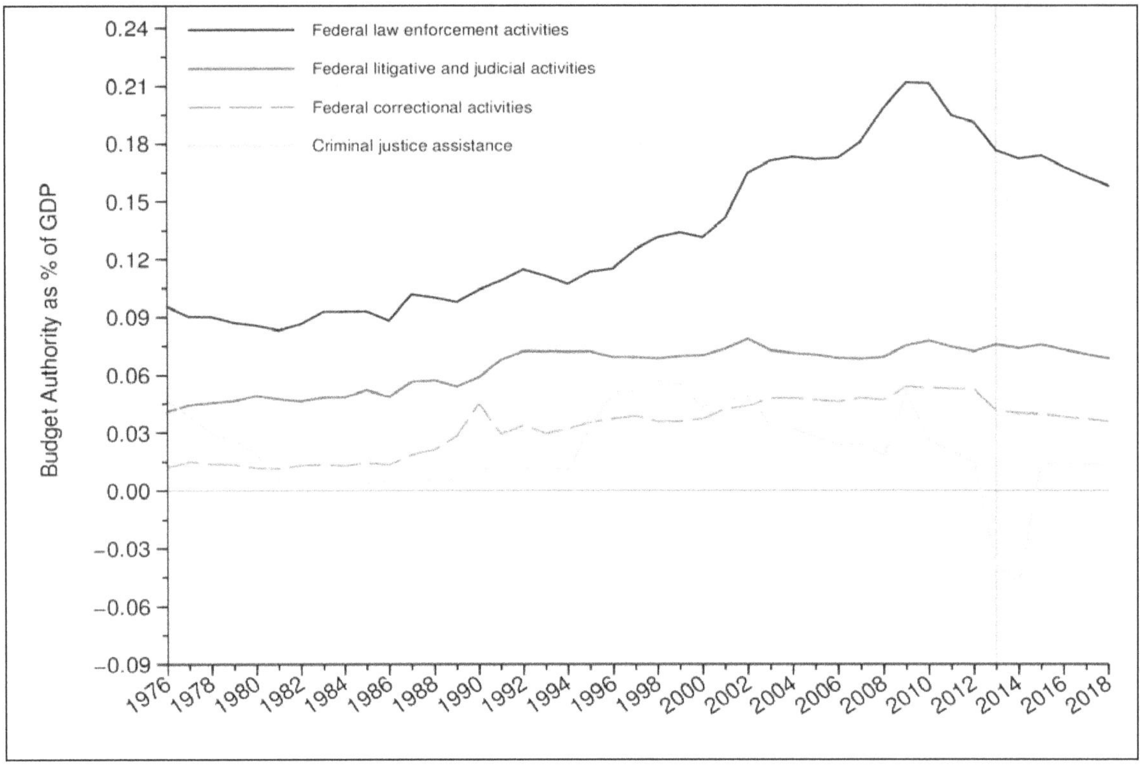

Source: CRS, based on OMB data from FY2014 budget submission.

Notes: FY2014-FY2018 levels reflect Administration proposals and projections. See OMB budget documents for further caveats.

Figure 18. General Government (800) Subfunctions

Discretionary budget authority as a percentage of GDP, FY1976-FY2018

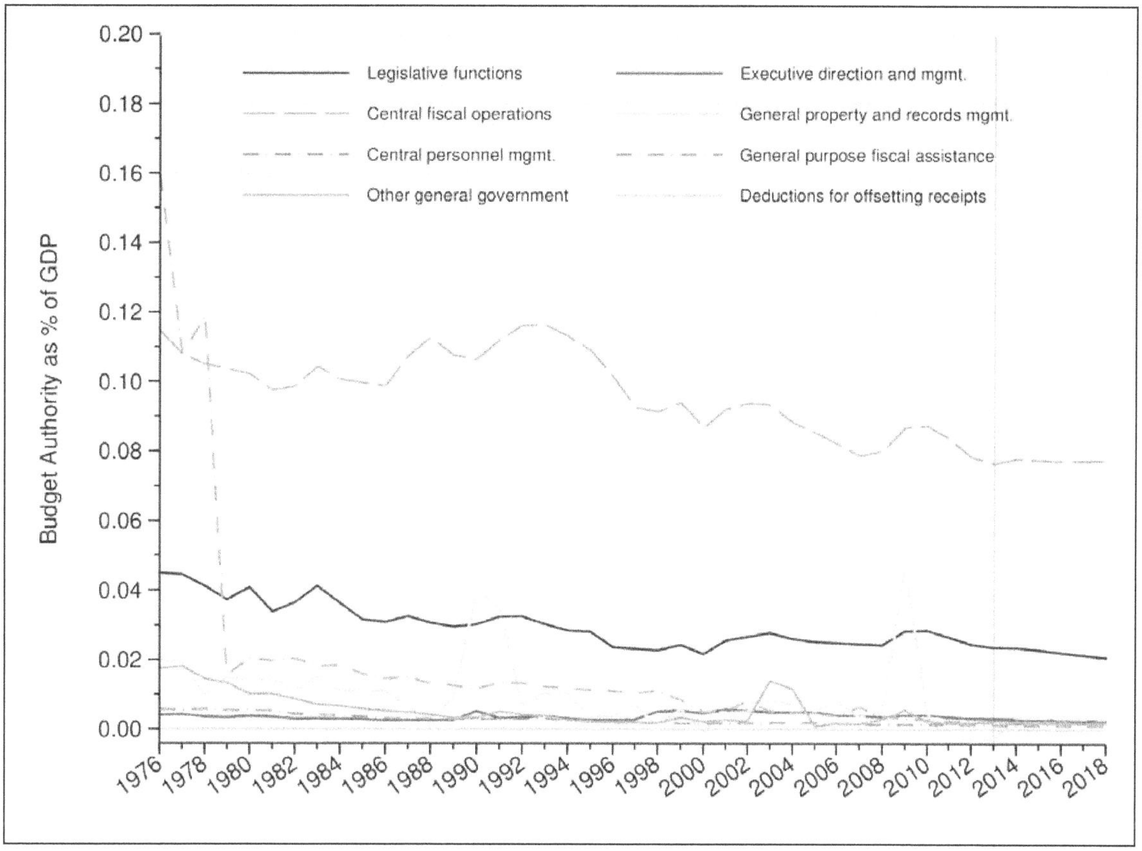

Source: CRS, based on OMB data from FY2014 budget submission.

Notes: FY2014-FY2018 levels reflect Administration proposals and projections. See OMB budget documents for further caveats.

Author Contact Information

D. Andrew Austin
Analyst in Economic Policy
aaustin@crs.loc.gov, 7-6552